The Hitler Youth

Marching Toward Madness

Many European countries were economically shattered and socially
unstable following World War I. For some, this sense of chaos,
combined with the Depression, contributed to a willingness to consider
extreme ideas such as National Socialism (Nazism). The map above shows
the war debts, in millions of dollars, owed by some European nations.

The Hitler Youth

Marching Toward Madness

by Alexa Dvorson

THE ROSEN PUBLISHING GROUP, INC.
NEW YORK

This book is dedicated to all who believe in telling the truth to make peace with the past, with themselves, and with one another.

Special thanks to Betty, Mel, Mimi, and Joshua Dvorson for their love and support; to Patra, for remembering me; and to Ulli and Edgar, for confiding in me.

Published in 1999 by The Rosen Publishing Group, Inc.
29 East 21st Street, New York, NY 10010

First Edition

Library of Congress Cataloging-in-Publication Data

Dvorson, Alexa.
The Hitler Youth : marching toward madness / by Alexa Dvorson.
  p. cm.
Includes bibliographical references and index.
Summary: Describes how many young Germans were drawn into the Nazi movement and how Germany came more and more under the total control of Hitler and the Nazis.
ISBN 0-8239-2783-0
1. Hitler-Jugend—Juvenile literature. 2. National socialism— Juvenile literature. 3. Germany—Politics and government—1933–1945— Juvenile literature. [1. Hitler Youth. 2. National socialism. 3. Germany—Politics and government—1933–1945.] I. Title.
DD253.5.D86 1999
943.086'083—dc21
          98-29025
          CIP
          AC

Manufactured in the United States of America

Contents

Introduction

It is important for everyone to learn about the Holocaust, the systematic murder of 6 million Jews during World War II (1939–1945). It is a dark scar across the face of human history. As a student, you are part of the future generation that will lead and guide the family of humankind. Your proper understanding of the Holocaust is essential. You will learn its lessons. You will be able to ensure that a Holocaust will never happen again and that the world will be a safe place for each person—regardless of his or her nationality, religion, or ethnicity.

Nazi Germany added a dangerous new element to the familiar concept of "dislike of the unlike." The Nazis introduced the idea that an *ethnic group* whom someone dislikes or hates can be isolated from the rest of the population and earmarked for total destruction, *without any possibility of survival.*

The Nazis chose the Jewish people for this fatal annihilation. Their definition of a Jew was a uniquely racial one: a person with Jewish blood. To the Nazis, a person with even one Jewish grandparent was a Jew—a person to be killed.

The Germans systematically rounded up Jews in the countries that they occupied during World War II. They built death camps equipped with the most sophisticated technology available in order to kill the Jews. With the assistance of collaborators (non-Germans who willingly helped), they murdered more than 6 million Jews. Among the victims were 1.5 million children and teenagers. These Jewish children, like Jewish adults, had no options. They were murdered because they had Jewish blood, and nothing they could do could change that.

Such a thing had never happened before in recorded history, despite the fact that genocide (deliberate destruction of people of one ethnic, political, or cultural group) had occurred. In the past, victims or oppressed people were usually offered an option to avoid death: they could change their religion, or be expelled to another country. But the Nazi concept of racism did not give the victim any possibility for survival, since a person cannot change his or her blood, skin color, or eye color.

Background photo: Pages from the achievement book that was given to members of the Hitlerjugend, or Hitler Youth.

A few non-Jewish people, known as the Righteous Among the Nations, saved Jews from death. They felt that they were their brothers' and sisters' keepers. But they were in the minority. The majority were collaborators or bystanders. During the Holocaust, I was a young child saved by several Righteous Poles. The majority of my family and the Jews of my town, many of whose families had lived there for 900 years, were murdered by the Nazis with the assistance of local collaborators. Photographs of those who were murdered gaze upon visitors to the Tower of Life exhibit that I designed for the United States Holocaust Memorial Museum in Washington, D.C.

We must learn the lessons of the Holocaust. We must learn to respect one another, regardless of differences in religion, ethnicity, or race, since we all belong to the family of humankind. The United States and Canada are both countries of immigrants, populated by many ethnic groups. In lands of such diversity, dislike of the unlike—the Nazi idea of using racial classification as a reason to destroy other humans—is dangerous to all of us. If we allow intolerance toward one group of people today, any of us could be part of a group selected for destruction tomorrow. Understanding and respecting one another regardless of religion, race, or ethnicity, is essential for coexistence and survival.

In this book individuals who were teenagers during the Holocaust share their experiences of life before and during the war and of the days of liberation. Their messages about their families, friends, love, suffering, survival, liberation, and rebuilding of new lives are deeply inspiring. They are important because these survivors are among the last eyewitnesses, the last links to what happened during the Holocaust.

I hope that their stories will encourage you to build a better, safer future "with liberty and justice for all."

Yaffa Eliach, Ph.D.
Professor of History and Literature
Department of Judaic Studies, Brooklyn College

Author's Note

This book tells the story of one German individual who willingly joined the Hitler Youth as a child. While his experiences may bear many similarities to those of other young Germans at the time, this portrayal does not claim to be representative of all members of the Hitler Youth. These are personal accounts.

chapter one

A Fateful Glimpse

One April afternoon, seven-year-old Edgar Gielsdorf was playing with his friend Alfred, who lived just a few doors away from a regional courthouse in the German city of Cologne. Suddenly he noticed something unusual going on. Groups of men stood talking outside the building in loud, angry tones; at the main entrance to the courthouse stood a crowd of uniformed Nazi storm troopers and policemen.

But what really caught the young boy's eye was a mass of garbage trucks parked in the courthouse's circular driveway. On

Opposite: Aerial view of Cologne, Germany, before the war.

Edgar and his mother.

the back of each truck, behind low metal grating one might see in an animal cage, Edgar saw a mass of well-dressed men shoved together, holding on to one another to keep those on the edge from falling out. Then he saw how more and more of these men were being dragged out of the courthouse by the stormtroopers and violently pushed onto other trucks.

Edgar understood from adults talking nearby that these men were judges, lawyers, and district attorneys. They were all Jewish. He had a queasy feeling in his stomach as he watched them being kicked and cursed, beaten and shoved by the stormtroopers. The feeling grew worse when the trucks pulled away from the courthouse and drove off, taking the Jews away.

But when Edgar got home and told his mother about it, she didn't seem too concerned. To her this was a political event, and since

German men and boys pose beneath a banner that reads, "Help liberate Germany from Jewish capital. Don't shop at Jewish-owned stores."

politics were not regarded as women's affairs in those days, it seemed none of her business.

It was three months since Adolf Hitler had come to power in Germany, and on this day, the first of April, 1933, he had proclaimed a boycott of all Jewish shops and businesses. It wasn't long before all Jews holding positions in schools, universities, hospitals, and cultural institutions were removed from their jobs and banned from seeking new ones in these professions.

There was another reason why Edgar's mother didn't react with more alarm when he came home with his dreadful story that day.

Even before Hitler took over, a hostile attitude toward Jews had been spreading throughout the country. During his many speeches, which were broadcast on loudspeakers set up in large public squares, Hitler claimed Jews were to blame for Germany's main woes: poverty, unemployment, and inflation. In fact, Jews had made significant contributions in nearly every aspect of German society. But Hitler used a harsh German word to condemn them: *Volksschädling*, or "pest of the people." He promised that all Germans' problems would vanish when he got rid of the Jews.

Edgar's father had once taken him by bicycle to one of these open-air gatherings at a public square near his home. The child was too young to understand much of Hitler's message, but he noticed that many people in the crowd—mostly men—would glance at each other with serious expressions during Hitler's frenzied speeches. They nodded in agreement and repeated certain key words Hitler uttered with his emphatic, choppy voice. It was all very impressive to the young boy.

He didn't know it then, but in several years' time, Edgar and hundreds of thousands of other German boys and girls would pledge their lives to the Nazi leader. They would become part of the Nazi organization for children known as the Hitler Youth. More than a decade would pass before Edgar realized how, as an enthusiastic leader of the Hitler Youth, he was manipulated, abused, and betrayed in the name of his country.

Members of the German League of Girls, one arm of the Hitler Youth, stand at attention to hear Hitler speak, 1932.

chapter two

Roots of Bitterness

Edgar Gielsdorf grew up like most other children in Germany. He loved playing with his friends in small public playgrounds or on the street. As in neighborhoods around the world, whenever a car was coming, they would yell "Car!" as a warning to get out of the way, and then resume their games of tag, cops and robbers, hide and seek, or hopscotch.

There was no money to go to the movies or buy toys. The most extravagant plaything anyone had was a ball, or crude wooden stilts fathers crafted for their children. But despite hard times, Edgar and his friends knew how to have fun. What mattered most to him was having a family and a place to come home to.

Though children like Edgar were somewhat shielded from the harsh reality of 1930s Germany, the Depression hit brutally hard. The currency was so devalued that it took at least a barrel of bills to equal a single U.S. dollar. With two-thirds of the population unemployed, poverty was rampant.

When Hitler came to power in 1933, Edgar's father had already been out of a job for seven years. In a country where hard work was highly respected and people often defined themselves by their professions, being jobless was almost as shameful as being in jail. At school, Edgar couldn't bring himself to admit that his parents were both unemployed.

Among the games Edgar and his friends liked to play was war. Edgar's father was a soldier in World War I, and though Germany had suffered a crushing defeat, people still spoke of their army with pride. Whenever Edgar listened to his father exchange war stories with other adults, the glory of being in the military was prevalent in their discussions, and it rubbed off on Edgar, who would later dream of going to war himself.

But in the meantime, the humiliation Germany suffered at the hands of France, Britain, and the United States had led to a deep resentment, which, along with the shattered economy, produced a bitter mood in the country. Germans were looking for someone or something to snap them out of it, and when Hitler took power, he appeared able to answer their every wish.

A Break from Loneliness

In another part of Cologne, a blond-haired, rosy cheeked girl named Ulli (OOH-lee) Lindener was too young to understand politics, but she could sense the misery in people's lives. She had no friends and felt lonely and restricted at home. Each day consisted of strict rules and routines. In those days of massive unemployment, her two parents were lucky to have jobs.

Ulli went to church almost every morning with her mother, who worked hard and didn't have much time or energy to entertain her only child with games or stories.

"That's why I went to the Hitler Youth," she explains. "It was so boring at home! There was nothing to do! No future! Hitler rescued everyone from joblessness and 'nobody-ness.'"

When Ulli was twelve, her schoolmates told her about a group of some twenty young girls who met every Wednesday and Saturday afternoon, just a few minutes' walk from where she lived. It sounded like the perfect way to escape her dreary days at home. At

Ulli in grade school.

15

the Hitler Youth group for young girls, or Jungen Mädel, they could sing and read books. They learned games indoors and later played them outside, including sports. Someone always provided a play space and a ball, a real luxury in those times. The Jungen Mädel group was part of the larger Bund Deutscher Mädel or BDM (German League of Girls), the Hitler Youth organization for girls.

"It was so much *fun*!" Ulli pronounces the word as though recalling some hidden treasure. She remembers their *Führerin*, or group leader, as a slightly older girl who had an authoritative personality but was especially nice to them. "She wasn't strict with us at all. She read to us. She loved us."

Lessons in Hatred

Along with hard work, one of the principal values in German society was obedience to authority. Everyone had someone to answer to, whether it was a parent, a boss, or a policeman. To the vast majority of Germans, strict obedience to one's superiors was second nature. It was not something to be questioned.

This was especially the case at school, where teachers represented the figure of authority and children were repeatedly punished if they disobeyed orders or otherwise misbehaved. Edgar typically saw classmates' faces or palms slapped, cheeks pinched or ears pulled if they were out of line. Even left-handed children were forced to use their right hands to write, because left-handedness was seen as wrong and going against the norm.

So when seven-year-old Edgar had antisemitic propaganda drummed into him by his teacher for the two months leading up to the Jewish boycott of April 1, 1933, he didn't think to oppose it, even though he had a couple of Jewish friends in his neighborhood. His teacher was an outspoken Nazi, and Edgar recalls how he and his schoolmates were taught they should hate Jews—as if this were as much a part of their lesson plan as math and grammar.

Edgar's father also sympathized with Nazi ideology. He and his friends who had served in the First World War were concerned that

League of German Girls members at play in the Rudolf Hess hospital, Dresden, Germany, December 10, 1936.

Lehrer an die Front!

Ein Brief, der uns Freude machte

Köln, den 24. 5. 35.

Sehr geehrter Pg. Streicher!

Ich darf wohl annehmen, daß es für Sie immer eine Freude ist, zu wissen, daß auch unter der Lehrer[schaft] der Gedanke Raum gewinnt, Ihnen in dem furcht[bar]en Kampfe, den Sie gegen das Judentum führen, zu [helfen]. Nur wenn unsere Jugend restlos über die furcht[bar]e Gefahr aufgeklärt wird, die das internationale Ju[den]tum nicht nur für das deutsche Volk, sondern für die

Ihnen folgendes Erlebnis, das ich mit einem neun[jährigen] Schüler meiner Klasse hatte, zeigen.

Eines Tages kommt er zur Schule und erzählt: Herr Lehrer, gestern ging ich mit meiner Mutter spazier[en]. Auf einmal, als wir beim Kaufhof vorbeigehen, fällt meiner Mutter ein, daß sie notwendig einige Rölld[chen] Zwirn braucht. Sie will mir Geld geben, damit ich [im] Kaufhofe den Zwirn kaufe. Darauf habe ich mei[ner] Mutter gesagt: „Dahinein gehe ich nicht, das mußt [du] schon selber tun. Aber das sage ich dir, wenn du in [den]

[ge]samte weiße Rasse bedeutet, ist der Endsieg zu erwarten. [A]uch in Köln ist eine kleine Schar Lehrer vorhanden, die [i]n nachdrücklichster Weise Sie in dem Ringen mit der [W]eltpest unterstützen will.

Ich habe mir aus Ihrer herrlichen Kampfzeitung, [dem] „Stürmer", eine Reihe von Judenköpfen, die einst[mals] in Deutschland herrschen durften, ausgeschnitten und, wie Sie aus beiliegender Photographie ersehen, aufgezogen. Mit dieser Anschauungstafel versehen halte ich in allen oberen Klassen meiner Schule Vorträge über die Juden[frage]. Aber auch die Frauenschaft, HJ., BDM. haben schon die Vorträge gehört und waren davon begeistert. Wie tief der Gedanke schon Wurzeln geschlagen hat, dürfte

Kaufhof gehst, dann sage ich es morgen unserem Lehrer[.] Der läßt dich zur Schule kommen, da kannst du was e[r]leben."

Sollte Ihnen beiliegendes Bild gefallen, dann würde[n] sich meine Kinder sehr freuen, wenn Sie es im „Stürmer" veröffentlichen könnten. Ich bin der Ueberzeugung, da[ß] solche Bilder zum Nacheifern anregen.

Ihnen in dem heißen Ringen weiter stahlharte Nerve[n] wünschend verbleibt mit vielen Grüßen und

Heil Hitler!

Burkert Max, Schulleiter,
Köln-Ehrenfeld, Schule Overbeckstraße.

discipline, order, and security were lacking in society. National Socialism seemed to them the perfect way to restore Germany's honor and dignity. Like millions of Germans, he was convinced Hitler would stamp out unemployment, seen as the "hostage of the masses."

But Edgar remembers his father was also disturbed that his Jewish friends were ostracized merely for being Jewish, and he couldn't understand such hatred. "He had the same reaction as an adult that I had as a kid at the courthouse. But with a tone of resignation he would say, 'You can't make an omelet without breaking eggs.'"

Most parents had no objection to their children joining the Hitler Youth, and Edgar's mother was no exception. "She saw my involvement in the Hitler Jugend as nothing out of the ordinary," Edgar recalls. "All that bothered her was that I wasn't available to look after my siblings and help out more at home."

When he joined the Deutsche Jungvolk, the youngest division of the Hitler Youth, his entry to Nazism began. It would be twelve years before he would take off his uniform once and for all.

This page from Edgar's Hitler Youth achievement book, which he received at age eight, includes a photograph of him in his Hitler Youth uniform.

Opposite: In Nazi Germany, the classroom became a place in which Hitler's ideas were regularly taught.

chapter three

A Sense of Belonging

A whole new world opened for children like Edgar and Ulli once they joined the Hitler Youth, or Hitler Jugend.

Twice a week, Edgar took part in organized sports, games, and outdoor training exercises such as map and compass reading. He learned many new songs whose words gave him and the other youngsters a sense of pride and camaraderie. They sang often, especially on hiking and camping trips. In his new uniform of short black pants, brown shirt, and black scarf around his collar with special insignia sewn on his sleeve, Edgar felt a sense of belonging to something strong and powerful. For him, the best part was that membership was free for children whose parents were unemployed.

Ulli told her parents right away that she was going to the Jungen Mädel twice a week. "My parents were reluctant. They would rather I'd gone to church. And I did! But this didn't have anything to do with church. We would walk in formation all the time, play ball and other games. I was so happy to be with girls of my age, to play with them, sing and read with them."

It all seemed innocent to Ulli's twelve-year-old mind. "We were

Hitler Youth members stand in formation during an assembly, 1936.

taught to be strong healthy German girls, and then to be German women. In those days that meant to have children, raise a family, and keep things in order. That seemed perfectly normal."

But Geerte Murmann, who was older than both Edgar and Ulli, witnessed something very abnormal one morning in front of her apartment house on Mozart Street.

Kristallnacht

Geerte played piano in a music ensemble of the German League of Girls. She was about to leave for school on the morning of November 10, 1938. This is what she remembers: "We suddenly saw clouds of smoke over the backyard and flames bursting from the synagogue on Roon Street. The rear courtyard of the synagogue was nearly joined to our own backyard. So we were close neighbors. My mother ran to the telephone booth on the street to call the fire department but couldn't get through.

"Just after 7:30 I got on my bicycle and rode to school like I did every day. Excitement reigned in the city. I saw shattered storefront windows of Jewish shops and clouds of smoke over the synagogue in the main part of town. It dawned on me that it could

The Fasanenstrasse synagogue in Berlin, Germany, burns during Kristallnacht, Nov. 10, 1938.

hardly be a coincidence that two synagogues were on fire at once. Not even the most naive observer could believe the newspapers' version of a 'spontaneous people's rage.'"

The ninth of November is now referred to as Kristallnacht, or "the night of broken glass," when approximately 100 Jews were killed, 30,000 Jewish men were arrested and sent to concentration camps, and synagogues throughout Germany and Austria were destroyed.

When Geerte arrived at school the next day, she had a strange encounter in class.

"We had first period with a teacher named Dr. Neuhaus, the only one of my instructors who appeared to show sympathetic feelings toward the Nazis. He came beaming into the classroom saying, 'Heil Hitler, eh?' We looked at him, taken aback.

"'Well, did you see it burning, the little fire at the synagogue?' he asked.

"We were speechless. Even our group leader of the German League of Girls entered in silence. We were upset, frightened, and apprehensive; no one was pleased by the events. Then he cheerfully asked two or three pupils: 'Ursula, Renate, did you see it?' They answered curtly, one after the other, 'Yes.' That was it. Nothing more. No one came to his aid. At that point he returned to the textbook and got on with the lesson."

Men to the Front, Women to the Nursery

The Hitler Youth was a highly structured organization made up of a hierarchy of subgroups, not unlike the military. They were divided according to age; each group was led by slightly older youngsters. The girls' group wore uniforms too: a blue skirt, a white blouse, and a brown jacket Ulli remembers as honey-colored. But she had none because her parents couldn't afford to buy her a uniform.

Whenever a rally or some other public gathering was scheduled, various subdivisions of both boys' and girls' Hitler Youth groups would march in formation with great fanfare and drum playing. Sometimes school classes were cancelled so the children could take part in these events. Whenever the national anthem was played, the youth always sang it with the Hitler salute: the right arm stretched forward, palm

Hitler Youth members saluting.

down. Edgar got goosebumps every time. He felt a triumph of
enthusiasm and dedication. He remembers such moments as "a
celebration of our generation."

But the real strategy behind all the organized activities for the
young boys was to prepare them for the military. Girls, meanwhile,
were instructed to grant Hitler's wish to bear many children for the
next generation of the "master race."

Both boys and girls in the Hitler Youth were taught that physical
fitness was not a private matter left to the individual. It was part of
the Nazi ideology. As Edgar's scout achievement booklet declared,
"Your body belongs to your nation, for you owe your very existence
to it." With this orientation, simple athletic activities like the high
jump, ball playing, and spear and disc throwing had much greater

As part of their training in the Hitler
Youth, many teenage boys were taught to
kill without remorse. One practice was to
have each boy bring a favorite pet to a
Hitler Youth meeting. There he was required
to kill it. In this way boys were trained
to believe that their obedience to Hitler
should outweigh their attachment to anyone
or anything else.

meaning. To the children in the Hitler Youth, fitness and sports
took on an almost sacred dimension, because they had a larger
purpose: the youth must be fit one day to serve their nation as
soldiers.

Love and loyalty toward the Fatherland, as Germany was always
called, were also central to Hitler Youth doctrine. After passing a
scout fitness achievement test in his fourth year of membership,
Edgar was initiated into the next order and given a scout knife
engraved with the phrase "blood and honor." His rite of passage
was accompanied by the words: "In this first test you fulfill your
duty for the first time. You do so with pleasure, because millions of
your young comrades do the same. You have become a soldier of
Adolf Hitler!"

Deutsche Sportjugend

Nürnberg, März 1937

26   Cover of a Hitler Youth publication entitled
German Sports Youth, dated March 1937.

Misguided Patriotism

Armed with his scout knife and an identity card with his picture on it, Edgar precisely fit the image of young boys Baldur von Schirach wanted when he was appointed leader of Germany's Hitler Youth in 1931. As Edgar eagerly climbed the ranks toward soldierhood, he heard many lectures and phrases that controlled his activities and influenced his world outlook. With such slogans as, "You are joyfully ready to die for your people in war," it was clear what Hitler and Baldur von Schirach were planning for all their obedient young men.

For girls, the message was more subtle. They learned idyllic songs about flowers, forests and streams. But Edgar was busy memorizing verses of a different nature. The fervent tone of the propaganda he heard inspired his eager devotion all the more, especially when the slogans were set to music:

> "Whether I return from war hardly matters,
>   what really counts is that my Fatherland is free."
> "Now let the flag fly in the great rosy dawn,
>   let it light our new victory, or burn us in death."

Every song, every group activity of the Hitler Youth was designed to instill a sense of self-worth that could be ultimately converted to national loyalty and willingness to live and die for Hitler. Edgar hoped that war wouldn't start before he was old enough to take part.

Adolf Hitler reviews troops in Nuremberg, Germany, September 1938.

chapter four

Mysterious Disappearances

In the midst of all his Hitler Youth activities, there was one thing no one seemed ready to talk about with Edgar. It was the disappearance of some of the people in his neighborhood. He started hearing about Mr. So-and-So being "picked up," and another Mr. So-and-So coming back but refusing to discuss what had happened to him. He also heard about someone else who had "gone into hiding because he was afraid of being taken away." Edgar was deeply confused by this. Yet whenever he asked what it all meant, where people were being taken and why, he never got an explanation.

Sometimes, after playing with his Jewish friend Oskar who lived a few doors away, he would attend a Hitler Youth meeting where people were chanting, "Hang the Jews!" But he wasn't too concerned.

Why didn't that upset him?

"That's a good question," he says today. "I don't have an answer. All I know is that I adjusted to it."

One day Oskar and his family disappeared, and Edgar had no idea where they went.

"At age thirteen or so, he and his parents moved away. They couldn't pay the rent in our neighborhood anymore. I thought about

A parade of Hitler Youth in Nuremberg, Germany, 1933.

him a lot, wondered what had happened to him. Then when I was sixteen, we heard Jews had been evacuated and resettled. This was seen as discrimination, but not life-threatening."

Edgar was too distracted by all the excitement in the Hitler Youth to give it much more thought. What he loved most were the torchlight marches and rallies, which included dancing by the League of German Girls, singing, and torch passing. At these events he heard that youth were "the most precious guarantee for a great future, destined to be the leaders of a glorious new order" under National Socialism.

Meanwhile, as Hitler's dictatorship set in, ordinary Germans lost most of their personal freedom. The "glorious new order" really meant *Gleichschaltung*: a society forced into line under one belief system, one lifestyle, and one leader, with no exceptions. One of Hitler's ultimate aims was a "thousand-year Reich," or reign, in which Germans, whom he saw as the master race, would rule the world for 1,000 years.

Any opposition to the Nazis was punished. The Hitler Youth were so effectively indoctrinated in their devotion that they even turned in members of their own family or neighbors if they heard anyone speaking out against Hitler. Punishment was severe. Many Germans who organized pockets of resistance were imprisoned; others were sent to concentration camps merely for opposing his politics out loud. Still others were executed.

So while Hitler ruled with an iron hand and eventually produced a climate of terror for adults, the children of the Hitler Youth seemed to live in a different world, a world of personal and national pride, of dreams and aspirations. Hitler had brainwashed them into thinking the "thousand-year Reich" meant they would one day rule the globe. This belief was reflected in the youths' favorite refrain: "Today Germany belongs to us, and tomorrow the whole world."

Germany Begins World War II

After annexing Austria and the former Czechoslovakia to become part of the new "Greater Germany," Hitler's army invaded Poland in September 1939, and Nazi occupation of Europe began. Geerte Murmann remembers that day clearly.

"At noon on the first of September, 1939, I went through the main shopping district, where a loudspeaker blasted Hitler's speech about the start of the war with these now famous words: 'Since this morning, we're firing back.'

"All through the area, I remember precisely, was dead

Once war began, the Nazis forced the Jews in German-occupied lands to leave their homes and move into overcrowded ghettos. Jews move their belongings into the Cracow ghetto in horse-drawn wagons, Cracow, Poland 1940.

silence. I knew that when World War I broke out, there was great celebration. What a contrast! The people who stopped to listen to Hitler's words were quiet and looked depressed. At home the mood was somber too, and my girls' group seemed helpless. No one had really expected a war to break out at this point. In any case this meant that soon—thank goodness—the most important thing to deal with now was handing out gas masks."

Since she was a member of the BDM, distribution of gas masks became a daily job for Geerte, as for the other members of her group.

"This meant guessing people's head size and fitting them, chin first, with a mask," she explained. "We'd say to them cheerfully, 'Just right,' or 'Wow, what a great fit!' Kids got children's masks. For grownups there were two sizes, as far as I can remember. Elderly women were hardest to deal with. There were always some who would complain it pulled their hair and they felt suffocated. Even in my dreams I was pulling gas masks over people's heads—people with big, small, fat, rosy or pale-cheeked faces.

"Generally, there wasn't much talk. People were rather dazed by the new situation, but somewhat thankful that the Nazi party apparently provided for them at times like this."

Preparing the Troops

By 1940, the National Youth Directorate ordered target practice and terrain maneuvers in addition to sports training for Hitler Youth boys age ten and over. Half a million boys received this training during the next two years. By the end of 1940, Edgar had fulfilled all the conditions for target

A German family is outfitted with gas masks after Germany declares war, 1939.

As the war intensified, so did the antisemitic propaganda in the Hitler Youth. They were told that, as members of the master race, they could not have anything to do with Jews and that they had to "help build a new Reich and stay loyal to their last breath." There was even a list of Ten Commandments for Marriage which all Hitler Youth boys and girls were expected to obey. Here are three of them.

- Remember you are a German.
- As a German, choose only a German spouse or someone with Nordic blood.
- When you've made a choice of a partner, ask about his or her ancestors.

But before they would even have a chance to marry, tens of thousands of Hitler Youth who fought as young soldiers would die in fierce fighting with the Russian army on the eastern front. Hundreds more committed suicide to die for their Führer with honor rather than be taken prisoner by the enemy.

practice, and a year after that he won an award for sharpshooting.

As he grew older, Edgar was recruited to lead a division of Hitler Youth. By the time he was seventeen, he was in charge of several divisions totalling 8,000 boys and girls. While it was unusual that someone that young would be responsible for so many youngsters, he took the job with pride and swore he would be a Hitler Youth leader for the rest of his life.

For the most part, these youth were not aware of how Hitler's Germany shook the world. The Nazis' absolute control of the media played a major role in keeping many Germans uninformed about the existence of death camps, where millions of Jews, along with members of the Roma and Sinti ethnic minority (also known as "Gypsies") were eventually sent.

Yet despite the fact that they saw people being rounded up and sent away, many Germans simply believed in their leader. They trusted that Hitler would do no wrong.

chapter five

Falling Bombs

While Germany was expanding its
reign of terror around Europe, the Allies (Britain, France, the
United States, and the Soviet Union) were bombing German cities.
Although civilians were killed, many young people found the raids
thrilling. Geerte Murmann wrote in her memoirs:

> The first bombs in Cologne were a sensation. Angry reactions
> from the youth were unheard of. They were excited by the whole
> disaster. Kids looked for pieces of shrapnel and traded them for
> anti-aircraft shells and other fragments. I was in Bavaria when

From 1939 until 1944, the German army appeared to be winning the war.
The Allies responded by bombing German cities. Above, hundreds of
German soldiers march, bearing Nazi banners.

the first bombs fell in Cologne. . . . I wrote my friend a letter full of disappointment: "Finally something terrific is happening in Cologne, and I'm not there."

Geerte isn't sure whether such immature expression was typical for young, innocent people at that time. She hungered for more bombing adventures and ultimately had her fill of them on trips to Berlin and Vienna. This is what she remembers from one air raid in Cologne:

"There were about fifty of us in a small bomb shelter—it was apparently next to another one at the Opera House. Above us was mostly air—it was not an ideal place to be during a bomb attack. After about a half hour the door flew open. A woman in a bathrobe surrounded by a cloud of dust from the rubble came in with a down quilt over her arm and a birdcage with a chirping canary inside. 'Everything's burning,' she cried. 'The whole street. Everything's on fire.'

"But just then there was an earsplitting noise, and no one had the courage to go outside and look. Around three in the morning came the all clear signal. A friend accompanied me back to our house on Mozart Street and then rushed home to his mother, who lived near the train station. Almost every house was on fire, and on the street we had to be careful to avoid being hit by falling, burning rubble.

"Mostly it was just the roofs that were burning," she continued, "nothing to compare with the firestorms that swept through Hamburg or Dresden, where people who fled landed in streets that had become whole rivers of fire. The wind blew particles of ash in our faces until our eyes teared and we looked like chimney sweepers. In front of our house lay beds, furniture, and suitcases in wild disarray. My mother had already thrown our down quilt out the window. The flames raged in the frame of the house, and our stone knight that ornamented the roof made a gruesomely beautiful silhouette against the blaze."

Mass Murder

By now Germany had invaded and occupied Denmark, Norway, Belgium, the Netherlands, Luxembourg, and France. In January 1942, Nazi leaders mapped out what they called the "Final Solution of the Jewish Problem" at the Wannsee Conference near Berlin. The

German troops cross the Meuse river to take Wadelincourt, France, May 1940, during the Nazi invasion of France.

plan was to round up Jews from all over Europe and deport them to death camps, most of which were set up in Poland. Others were established in Germany, the former Soviet Union, and elsewhere in eastern Europe.

It wasn't only Jews who were deported. Other prisoners included homosexuals, people in resistance to the Nazis, African Germans, and members of the Sinti and Roma ethnic minority. Once the deportees arrived at the camps, doctors divided them into two groups. Those deemed healthy enough to work became slave laborers, and those considered too weak to work were exterminated in gas chambers soon after arriving. Most of those who were forced to work in the camps were eventually killed. An estimated six million Jews were killed, as well as up to half a million Sinti and Roma. Out of millions of people deported to the camps, survivors numbered only in the thousands. Over one and a half million of those killed were children.

An operation of such massive dimensions took an extraordinary degree of organization and coordination, especially over such great distances, from one end of the continent to the other. For this the Nazis relied on hundreds of thousands of ordinary Germans to help them carry out the tasks of searching for Jews who were in hiding, notifying those who were still living in their homes, rounding them up, seizing their property, and putting them on trains bound for the camps. The amount of paperwork involved was staggering, but the operation proceeded efficiently and at considerable speed. Thus the train drivers, secretaries, police, city officials, and other administrators all played a role in helping the Nazis fulfill Hitler's planned genocide.

The Power of Lies

The mood in Germany began to change as hardship intensified during the war, but boys and girls in the Hitler Youth were led to believe it was all for a grand purpose.

Edgar, now seventeen, worked as a Hitler Youth leader of a division called a *Bann*, which was made up of five or six subgroups called *Unterbanne*. His position as *Bannführer* was the military

Children imprisoned in Auschwitz concentration camp look out
from behind a barbed wire fence.

equivalent of Major-General. He now had permission to carry a gun
on his uniform, which made him feel proud and very important.

Edgar knew nothing about the death camps. He was aware that
Jews, Roma, and Sinti were being "taken away somewhere," but he
didn't know much beyond that. Like millions of other Germans, he had
been conditioned to concentrate merely on following orders and not to
question authority.

What Edgar did know was that in 1943, two years after invading
Russia, the Germans suffered a horrendous military defeat. But he
didn't realize that after losing two-thirds of their soldiers, they had
surrendered to the Russian army. This was because the Nazis never
broadcast this information on the radio.

From time to time Edgar listened to broadcasts from other
countries on shortwave radio, even though that was illegal under the
Nazis. Although he heard things that contradicted German radio, he
dismissed it as "enemy propaganda." It never occurred to him to
regard the Nazi broadcasts as anything other than the truth.

Even Edgar's father, whose loyalty to the Nazis had begun to

Dr. Joseph Goebbels

(1897-1945), Reich Minister for Public Enlightenment and Propaganda, was a student of literature and drama. In 1926 Goebbels showcased his theatrical vehemence in speeches to unemployed Germans, in which he blamed Jews for Germany's economic problems. He was a master of words. In 1933 Goebbels distributed radios to citizens so they could listen to Hitler's radio broadcasts. He staged the public book burnings of May 1933 and help organize Kristallnacht in 1938. He played an important part in creating the image of the Nazi ideal that captivated the Hitler Youth. Hitler admired Goebbels and sought his counsel. In July 1944, Goebbels became General Plenipotentiary for Total War even though he had been rejected from the army for having a deformed leg.

Hitler's obsession with preserving the master race also extended to "weeding out" members of German society. Hitler established a program to sterilize all adults with mental or physical disabilities to prevent them from giving birth to disabled children who did not fit the Nazis' vision of a "strong and able-bodied nation." But unlike the mass murder of Jews, the sterilization program was not something the Nazis tried to keep a secret. They even took Hitler Youth groups on "field trips" to hospitals and institutions to impress upon them how much of a financial "burden" mentally disabled people imposed on German society. In one edition of the Hitler Youth newsletter, *You and Your People,* a justification for the sterilization program was given:

"You should produce children only with pure Germans to avoid bringing criminals or disabled people into the world. The sterilization law allows us to . . . exercise human dignity and not subject our race to inferiority. . . ."

How did Edgar react to this policy?

He thought it was correct. When he accompanied the Hitler Youth to a mental institution and had a glimpse of the inmates, he felt that these kind of people were a "disgrace to the race." As if acting on orders, he spread the word and promoted the sterilization plan based on what he'd seen.

Some years later, Edgar found out that some 130,000 disabled children and adults were put to death by Nazi doctors because they were considered "useless" to society. This brutal chapter of Nazi terror still haunts Germany today.

wane, couldn't convey his doubts about the outcome of the war to his son with any effect. Edgar still believed what he heard on the radio—that everything was going fine, and Germany would be victorious. He was glad he would soon become a soldier.

Induction

Eventually the day came when, instead of playing soldiers as they did when they were children, Edgar and his comrades put on uniforms and became soldiers themselves. Military order was no longer just a game, but a reality.

Until now, the fanatic enthusiasm of the Germans had been at a high point. But gradually, Edgar began to sense that the Nazis' *Kriegsgluck*, or war luck, had begun to run out. People with similar views started discussing it more, but never dared to doubt the Nazis in public. "It was instant death for anyone who expressed such things openly," says Edgar.

By the end of 1943, Hitler's notorious security forces, known as the SS, had established the Female Assistance Corps. Although Hitler's principal vision for women was to have as many children as possible for the "master race," girls in the BDM were now recruited to the military as the war intensified. The real purpose of these women's battalions was to shame men and boys into fighting harder.

At this point, every boy of seventeen was receiving premilitary training in one of the 226 Hitler Youth fitness camps set up throughout Germany. By early 1944, the mood in the country had changed noticeably. The Hitler Youth proclaimed it the "Year of the War Volunteer," but in fact young Germans had no choice; they were now ordered to volunteer for the armed forces.

Edgar was among those stationed in the military fitness camps.

chapter six

A Rude Surprise

In 1944 the German war effort grew even more desperate. The Nazi empire was shrinking. So many German troops had died fighting the Allies that adult manpower was in short supply. The SS soldiers drew almost all their recruits from the Hitler Youth, drafting fifteen and sixteen year-olds.

In addition, men originally considered too old to serve were also drafted into an army division called the *Volkssturm,* or "people's assault." Boys as young as eleven were assigned to handle anti-tank weapons, and girls were called on to staff anti-aircraft batteries. Anyone who deserted the *Volkssturm* could be shot.

At the end of November that year, Edgar was on the former Polish-Czechoslovak border with two other soldiers, discussing various medals awarded to the wounded. Suddenly, his two comrades were knocked flat on the ground. Edgar had not heard the quiet hiss of a grenade but saw an explosion several yards away. Then he felt a banging blow in his thigh. He could have been killed, but after he realized what happened, his first thought was: "Now I'll get a special badge for the war-wounded!"

Today Edgar considers this kind of thinking crazy. But at the time, it was completely in line with the way Hitler Youth were programmed to behave as war heroes.

Fortunately, a surgeon was able to cut out most of the deadly shell splinter in his leg. Edgar had nearly lost a limb. But once off the operating table, he could hardly wait to get back to the Hitler Youth.

Hope vs. Dread

Edgar now walked with a cane. He was given a transfer to receive treatment with replacement troops in Bremen. His father came and joined him for the ride back home. With almost no train connections, they had to walk or ride in open trucks, always under low-flying attacks by American bombing fleets. Today the distance between Bremen and Cologne can be covered in about three hours, but in the drastic conditions of the war, it took them four days. They spent nights in overcrowded air raid shelters.

Edgar didn't stay home long. He hurried back to Bremen only to discover that the other troops had left for a training course. There were new superiors whom Edgar didn't know, and it was clear they didn't need "heroes" like Edgar in his wounded state. He was shipped off to a recovery camp near Dresden.

In mid-February 1945, Edgar returned home once more on recovery leave. The city looked desolate. Artillery from both sides of the fighting could be heard, and the city looked set to become a war front. Edgar's father was afraid of getting drafted into the *Volkssturm* at the last moment and considered breaking his teeth as an excuse not to go. As much as Edgar loved him and wanted him to survive, he couldn't understand this attitude. He still believed in victory for Germany.

"But for my father it was all over, the war *and* National Socialism!" says Edgar. "There were horrible days at home. Neither of us could convince the other. It was a terrible vacation."

Edgar's father was worried about his son's future after the war. "What will you do for a living?" he asked.

Without missing a beat, Edgar replied, "I will never take off these boots, whether as a Hitler Youth leader or as an officer. My life still belongs to Hitler!"

"Stay here and turn yourself in, go to jail, or just hide!" his father pleaded. But Edgar would hear none of it. After two weeks he left to catch up with his recovery unit. He could not conceive of his own father advising him to desert the army.

On his way back to Dresden, Edgar finally got a glimpse of Germany's "wonder weapons"—planes that could fly two or three times faster than previously imaginable. Now that he had seen them with his own eyes, he was even more convinced that Germany could still win the war, even at the last minute.

chapter seven

In the spring of 1945, Edgar's understanding of the Nazis reached a turning point. About a week before the end of the war, he was dispatched westward with a group of fifty convalescing soldiers from a post near Dresden. On their way, they rounded a curve on a remote road and suddenly came to a stop.

Ahead Edgar saw a few unwashed, unshaven SS officers in dirty uniforms. They were visibly drunk and looked as though they had just emerged from a long and exhausting combat. Their faces were expressionless; they passed the convalescing soldiers without greeting them.

Edgar and his comrades were shocked to see that the officers were followed by about thirty-five Jewish women, recognizable by the yellow stars the Nazis had forced Jews to wear on their sleeves.

The women walked with their bodies hunched over, heads down. They seemed to focus only on putting one burdened foot in front of the other. Some wore old untied work shoes; others wore none at all, their feet wrapped only in old rags. A few had long coats, or mere cloth wrapped around their frail bodies. Their hair was unkempt; their cheeks were hollow. The commanders yelled at them, "Forward! Forward!"

"It was as though some giant tent had collapsed on us and took our breath away, as well as our ability even to think," Edgar remembers. "It was obvious, absolutely crystal clear what we were seeing. There were many times afterward that I couldn't eat. I could hardly grasp what was going on."

Edgar and his fellow soldiers had witnessed one of the many death marches the SS had led from the concentration camps in the final weeks of the war. Realizing the camps were about to be liberated by the Allied forces, the SS ordered the camps evacuated in an attempt to hide evidence of the genocide that had taken place. Although surviving prisoners were close to death already, they were forced to walk for days until many either dropped dead or were shot.

As Edgar watched this horrifying scene, he saw a few more SS underlings bringing up the rear, all with submachine guns. He remembers that his boss inquired about the group and was told, "This is the remainder of 300, but they're only going as far as the edge of the forest, then we'll get rid of them. They know it too."

The fact that these tortured beings were women was even more devastating to Edgar. "If this had been a group of men, it wouldn't have affected me nearly as much," he later recalled. "For me, women were something special. That's how I was brought up in those days, to regard women as the mothers of future children. To see them like this was sheer horror."

Edgar and his comrades were quiet for some time. After a mile or so, their commander resumed issuing orders to them.

This time Edgar found neither excuses nor explanations for what he had seen. He now understood the horrors he'd witnessed were not the deeds of only a few. He knew he had seen and heard the truth. In his unswaying devotion to Hitler, he had been marching toward madness.

chapter eight

No More Uniform

The Allied Forces fighting the Nazis were closing in on Germany. The Russians advanced from the east, and the French, British, and Americans had begun to occupy western Germany. Since Edgar was afraid he might be taken prisoner, he resolved to carry a pistol with him at all times. Now nineteen, he was ready to use it on himself rather than give victory to the enemy. "The gun was my last security," he later wrote.

Since he felt he was more of a target in uniform, he and a fellow soldier obtained some civilian clothes and set off for the western front. Soon after, they were relieved to reach a bridge guarded by the Americans, which meant they'd escaped the Russians.

The war ended with Hitler's suicide and Germany's unconditional surrender a week later. May 8, 1945, was a great day of victory and celebration for people around the world. Europeans felt they would never have to fear the Nazis again. Many Germans considered themselves liberated as well. Even as bombs fell on their own cities, some were glad to see Germany lose the war because it meant the end of Hitler's reign of terror.

But for Edgar and his comrades, May 8 meant absolute defeat.

American servicemen and servicewomen gather in front of the "Rainbow Corner" Red Cross club in Paris to celebrate the end of the war in Europe, May 8, 1945.

His time as a "hero" was over. He tossed his gun in a creek and shed his uniform once and for all.

After some conversation with his comrades, Edgar began walking alone. The feelings that had been stored up within him now churned uncontrollably in his mind. All the trauma he had encountered as a young soldier—the grenade attack, the women on the death march, and his shattered ideals at the end of the war—built up and threatened to overwhelm him.

To conquer this inner turmoil, he instinctively cut himself off from all his worries and concentrated on the moment at hand. This strategy worked. He was anxious to see his family again, so he set all his thoughts on getting home.

With this inner strength and the good luck of fair weather, Edgar's trek from east to west put him in high spirits. He had no identity papers, so to avoid being checked by the Americans, he took a route through fields and forests.

Being this close to nature was a great solace to him. Sleeping in the grass or strolling in the sun, he sensed a joy and a lightness he'd never known before. He suddenly felt unburdened with no one to answer to—no orders to follow, no responsibilities. All that mattered was to keep moving west. He instinctively felt whatever might happen, he would manage somehow.

It took Edgar three weeks to reach home. He had walked about 400 miles. When he arrived, he was so relieved to find his family alive and well that their material losses seemed unimportant. But his father told him, "You can't stay here. The Americans have already asked about you."

So Edgar had to flee again.

On the Run

It turned out that people in Edgar's neighborhood had denounced him as a Nazi. So he stayed just one night with his family and left the next day.

It was the end of May, 1945. Much of Germany lay in ruins. People were preoccupied with rebuilding their homes and cities. With streets, bridges, schools, and commerce districts reduced to rubble, sheer survival was an enormous struggle. Because so many families had been separated during the war, it seemed to Edgar that half of Germany was in transit that summer. Some were searching for lost relatives; others who had been evacuated were on their way back home.

Edgar wanted to avoid being asked if he'd served in the Hitler Youth. He knew if it came to that, he would tell the truth and be imprisoned. So he made up an alibi: *When he returned to Cologne as a soldier, he heard his family had been evacuated, so he was out to find them.* He spent nights in public shelters set up for those on the road. In mid-

Dresden, Germany, was devastated after the Allied bombardment of February 1945.

July, he met up with Egon, an old comrade from one of his military training courses. Egon's family urged him to stay at their home until he was "reunited with his own family."

Edgar found work for several months with the British occupying army in a former German munitions depot. In mid-November, all employees had to fill out a questionnaire. Edgar wrote the truth about his activities on the form, then left for Cologne.

The British authorities contacted his host family and gave an address where Edgar was asked to report and answer some questions. The next month, Edgar appeared as requested, and a year's internment began.

Relief and Regret

Edgar felt relieved to get the truth off his chest.

"I wanted clarity," he says today. "Whatever was going to happen to me as a result, I was ready. If I was going to be jailed or interned, then so be it. I didn't enjoy this life 'in between.' I always tried to be a sincere person. I wanted to tell the truth about what I was doing. I didn't want to keep making up all these stories . . ."

It was a simple procedure. "Are you Edgar Gielsdorf?" the authorities asked.

"Yes," came the reply.

"You were a Hitler Youth leader?"

"Yes."

That was it.

Edgar wasn't guilty of any real crime. But he had participated in the vast organizational network that enabled others to commit atrocities.

At the internment camp, Edgar took part in discussions with a group of young men his own age. This brought him to another level of awareness: all he had done and believed in as a member of the Hitler Youth was wrong. The realization that millions of youngsters had been betrayed triggered great anger and grief among the young men: they had given of themselves completely, and now their dream was dead.

Rebuilding from Rubble

Like millions of other Germans after the war, Ulli Lindener and her parents struggled to reshape their shattered lives. She returned to Cologne with her mother after staying in the countryside during the massive bombing raids. But unlike the internment camp, where Edgar had plenty of time to reflect on the truth about the Nazis, it was never discussed in Ulli's household. For her family, the Holocaust was yesterday's tragedy.

"That subject never came up," she says. "Of course it was awful—it was dreadful for everyone that something like this could happen, that millions of lives were lost. We choked on the knowledge of it. Life for us was a catastrophe. Whether you had been for or against the Nazis, now we were all stuck in the same rubble. We had to survive, to rebuild the country."

Throughout Germany, the occupying powers carried out the process of "denazification." At first they were afraid that underground Nazism in postwar Germany would be a threat. Great pains were taken to get former Nazis to confess to their acts and pledge to reform under the new system. But now that it was no longer acceptable to be associated with Hitler or the Nazis, few Germans were willing to acknowledge they had supported him or played any kind of role in his National Socialist order. Edgar says the fear of a new wave of Nazism was unfounded, because suddenly all the Nazis seemed not to exist.

"Nobody would admit to having done anything willingly!" he says in disgust. "They all said they acted under pressure. They were cowards in the biggest sense of the word, because they wouldn't stand up to what they had done."

Skeptics had only to point to the pictures of cheering masses who had applauded Hitler's every speech for more than a decade.

For Edgar, the "outer" process of denazification proved far easier than the inner process of cleansing away his old belief system. For him, the real punishment was the fact that he could not uproot his devotion to Hitler overnight and plant something new to replace it. It was much more complicated than merely taking off a uniform.

Background: Photos like this one of cheering Hitler Youth made it impossible for many Germans to deny their support of the Nazi cause.

Yet despite the outrage Edgar and the other internees felt at this sense of betrayal, the overwhelming emotion Edgar felt was one of relief that he finally understood the truth. He compared it to a mountain whose summit he thought he would never reach. His greatest battle was now within his own mind, which had been so manipulated and seduced by his Nazi leaders. He was finally on his way to reclaiming his own thinking.

Above: Aerial view of Cologne after World War II. More than 90 percent of the city was destroyed.

chapter nine

Release and Remorse

Edgar was released from the internment camp in November 1946. He was grateful to the British authorities who introduced him to democracy and helped open his eyes to the truth about Nazi Germany.

Now an elderly man with grandchildren, Edgar has dusted off his old notebooks to retrieve his memories. He wants his children and grandchildren to know about Germany's past so they will never take today's freedom and democracy for granted.

Today he compares the seduction-like effect of the Hitler Youth to a satanic pied piper, who put children under his spell by playing his flute. They only had to listen, and they would follow him anywhere. He describes it this way:

"The flute song had many verses. Sport was one, as was hiking, and the trips we took—everything that appealed to us as kids. They played just the right tune. We heard only this, and never did we hear the parents or other grown-ups who heard the bad notes, who warned us or tried to hold us back."

On a more painful note, he says: "When I think of the past, I really don't have feelings of guilt, but an enormous shame. I'm ashamed that I participated in the Hitler Youth. I'm ashamed that I was so dumb, that I followed these ideals, that I let them make their mark on me. I'm ashamed I was a part of it all, that I just didn't get it all that time! I'm ashamed that I was so dumb and went along with it."

Ulli Lindener is also troubled by her country's history. "It will always haunt us, this 'Thousand Year Reich.' It's horrible," she says today. "We've been dragging it with us in our memory ever since. We'll always have it at the back of our minds. We can't forget it, and we shouldn't."

To ensure that this kind of phenomenon can never happen again, Edgar Gielsdorf makes a simple plea: *Wehret den Anfängen:* Stop it before it starts.

Timeline

January 30, 1933	Adolf Hitler is appointed chancellor of Germany.
March 23, 1933	Dachau, the first concentration camp, is built to imprison political opponents of the Nazis.
April 1, 1933	Nazis proclaim a boycott of Jewish-owned businesses.
July 14, 1933	Nazis outlaw all other political parties in Germany; a law is passed legalizing forced sterilization of Roma and Sinti ("Gypsies"), mentally and physically disabled Germans, African-Germans, and others.
January 26, 1934	Germany and Poland sign Non-Aggression Pact.
August 1, 1935	"No Jews" signs begin to appear in Germany barring Jews from stores, restaurants, places of entertainment, etc.
September 15, 1935	German parliament passes the Nuremberg Laws, which revoked the citizenship of German Jews and took away many of their rights.
March 13, 1938	Germany annexes Austria.
September 29, 1938	Munich Conference: Britain and France allow Hitler to annex part of Czechoslovakia in order to prevent war.
November 9, 1938	Kristallnacht (looting and vandalism of Jewish homes businesses and widespread destruction of synagogues) occurs throughout Germany and Austria; 30,000 Jews are sent to Nazi concentration camps.
March 15, 1939	Germany invades all of Czechoslovakia.
August 23, 1939	Germany and Soviet Union sign Non-Aggression Pact.
September 1, 1939	Germany invades western Poland.
September 2, 1939	Great Britain and France declare war on Germany.

September 17, 1939	Soviet Union invades eastern Poland.
Spring 1940	Germany invades Denmark, Norway, Holland, Luxembourg, Belgium, and France.
March 24, 1941	Germany invades North Africa.
April 6, 1941	Germany invades Yugoslavia and Greece.
June 22, 1941	Germany invades western Soviet Union.
July 31, 1941	Reinhard Heydrich appointed to carry out the "Final Solution" (extermination of all European Jews).
Summer 1941	*Einsatzgruppen* (mobile killing squads) begin to massacre Jews in western Soviet Union.
December 7, 1941	Japan bombs Pearl Harbor; United States enters World War II.
January 20, 1942	Wannsee Conference: Nazi leaders meet to plan the "Final Solution."
Spring and Summer 1942	
	Many Polish ghettos emptied; residents deported to death camps.
February 2, 1943	German troops surrender in Stalingrad, Soviet Union; the Allies begin to win the war.
June 11, 1943	Nazis decide that all remaining ghettos in Poland and Soviet Union are to be emptied and residents deported to death camps.
March 19, 1944	Germany occupies Hungary.
June 6, 1944	D-Day: Normandy Invasion by the Allies.
January 30, 1945	Russian forces liberate Auschwitz concentration camp.
May 8, 1945	Germany surrenders to the Allies; war ends in Europe.

Glossary

Allied forces British, French, Soviet, and U.S. armies united in Europe to fight Nazi Germany during World War II.

antisemitism Hatred toward or bias against the Jewish people.

Bund Deutscher Mädel (German League of Girls) The Hitler Youth organization for girls.

collaborators Non-Germans who willingly helped or supported the Nazis.

concentration camp A camp where people are kept in inhumane conditions, and are killed by starvation, exhaustion, disease, torture, or execution.

death camp A camp set up to kill people and dispose of their bodies.

death march A forced march by camp inmates as the Germans tried to outrun the advancing Allied armies; most inmates did not survive the marches.

denazification The process by which former Nazis were made to confess to their acts and pledge to reform under the new system of democracy installed by the occupying Western Allies.

Final Solution The term used by the Nazis for their systematic plan to muder the entire Jewish population of Europe.

genocide The deliberate destruction of one ethnic, political, religious, or cultural group.

Hitler Youth The Nazi organization set up to integrate children into the war effort.

Holocaust The extermination of 6 million Jews by the Nazis.

ideology The beliefs held by an individual, group, or culture.

internment camp A camp where Nazi war criminals were held by Allied forces.

Jungen Mädel A Hitler Youth group for young girls.

Kristallnacht The Nazi-organized demonstration of violence against the Jews of Germany and Austria on the night of November 9, 1938.

Nazi The political party that ruled in Germany (1933–1945); full name: National Socialist German Workers' Party.

propaganda The spreading of ideas, information, lies, or rumor for the purpose of strengthening a cause or harming others.

storm troopers Members of a Nazi task force noted for aggressive behavior.

Third Reich A reign that the Nazis believed would last for 1,000 years.

Wannsee Conference The meeting at which the Nazis discussed plans for the "Final Solution"; held on January 20, 1942, in Berlin, Germany.

World War I The war in Europe that lasted from 1914 until 1918.

World War II The most devastating war in human history, lasting from 1939 until 1945 and involving countries all over the world.

For Further Reading

Altschuler, David A. *Hitler's War Against the Jews.* West Orange, NJ: Behrman House, 1978.

Drucker, Malka, and Michael Halperin. *Jacob's Rescue: A Holocaust Story.* New York: Bantam Doubleday Dell, 1993.

Eisenberg, Azriel. *The Lost Generation: Children in the Holocaust.* New York: Pilgrim Press, 1982.

Eliach, Yaffa. *Hasidic Tales of the Holocaust.* New York: Random House, 1988.

Frank, Anne. *Diary of a Young Girl: The Definitive Edition.* New York: Doubleday, 1995.

Holliday, Laurel. *Children in the Holocaust and World War II: Their Secret Diaries.* New York: Washington Square Press, 1994.

Jules, Jacqueline. *The Grey Striped Shirt: How Grandma and Grandpa Survived the Holocaust.* Los Angeles: Alef Design, 1994.

Klein, Gerda. *All but My Life.* New York: Hill & Wang, 1995.

Marks, Jane. *The Hidden Children: The Secret Survivors of the Holocaust.* New York: Ballantine Books, 1993.

Matas, Carol. *Daniel's Story.* New York: Simon and Schuster, 1996.

Rochman, Hazel, and Darlene Z. McCampbell, eds. *Bearing Witness: Stories of the Holocaust.* New York: Orchard Books Watts, 1995.

Roth-Hano, Renee. *Touch Wood.* New York: Puffin Books, 1989.

Wiesel, Elie. *Night.* New York: Bantam Books, 1982.

Wilkomirski, Benjamin. *Fragments.* New York: Schocken Books, 1996.

For Advanced Readers

Asscher-Pinkhof, Clara. *Star Children*. Detroit: Wayne State University Press, 1986.

Dwork, Deborah. *Children with a Star*. New Haven, CT: Yale University Press, 1991.

Edelheit, Abraham J., and Herschel Edelheit. *History of the Holocaust: A Handbook and Dictionary*. Boulder, CO: Westview Press, 1994.

Gilbert, Martin. *The Holocaust: A History of the Jews of Europe During the Second World War*. New York: Henry Holt & Co., 1985.

I Never Saw Another Butterfly: Children's Drawings and Poems from Theresienstadt Concentration Camp. New York: McGraw-Hill, 1964.

Noakes, J., and G. Pridham. *Nazism: A History in Documents and Eyewitness Accounts, Vols. I and II*. New York: Pantheon Books, 1984.

Videos

Heil Hitler! Confessions of a Hitler Youth
Former Hitler Youth Alfons Heck describes his experiences in Nazi Germany. Heck's story is supported by documentary footage that shows how Germany's youth were trained to be fanatically devoted to the Nazi cause. Heck is now a U. S. citizen and works to educate people about the Holocaust. (Available from Zenger Video, 10200 Jefferson Boulevard, P. O. Box 802, Culver City, CA 90232, (800) 421-4246.)

Hitler: The Whole Story
Using documentary footage, photographs, and interviews, this film provides an in-depth look at Hitler—his ideology and his actions. (Available from NDR International, Hitler Offer, P. O. Box 68618, Indianapolis, IN 46268, (800) 423-8800.)

Opening the Gates of Hell
American liberators share their memories of liberation. Interviews

are combined with photos and footage showing camps liberated by Americans: Buchenwald, Dachau, Landsberg, Mauthausen, and Nordhausen. Note: Highly graphic. (Available from Ergo Media, Inc., P. O. Box 2037, Teaneck, NJ 07666; (800) 695-3746.)

Safe Haven
This video profiles America's only refugee camp for victims of Nazi terror. Nearly 1,000 refugees were brought to Oswego, NY, and incarcerated in a camp known as Fort Ontario for eighteen months. (Available from the Anti-Defamation League, 823 United Nations Plaza, New York, NY 10017; (212) 885-7700.)

Shoah
This film includes interviews with victims, perpetrators, and bystanders, and takes viewers to camps, towns, and railways that were part of the Holocaust. (Available in most video stores and many libraries.)

Web Sites

Anti-Defamation League—Braun Holocaust Institute
http://www.adl.org/Braun/braun.htm

Holocaust Education and Memorial Centre of Toronto
http://www.feduja.org

Museum of Tolerance
www.wiesenthal.com/mot/index.html

Simon Wiesenthal Center
http://www.wiesenthal.com/

United States Holocaust Memorial Museum
http://www.ushmm.org/index.html

Yad Vashem
http://www.yad-vashem.org.il

Index

About the Author

Alexa Dvorson is a broadcast journalist from San Francisco who has lived in Cologne, Germany, since 1986. As a public radio correspondent, she has produced documentaries from eastern and western Europe, Alaska, Africa, and Nepal. She was recently awarded a Knight International Press Fellowship to offer media training overseas.

About the Series Editor

Yaffa Eliach is Professor of History and Literature in the Department of Judaic Studies at Brooklyn College. She founded and directed the Center for Holocaust Studies (now part of the Museum of Jewish Heritage—A Living Memorial to the Holocaust) and designed the Tower of Life exhibit at the U.S. Holocaust Memorial Museum. Professor Eliach is the author of *Hasidic Tales of the Holocaust; We Were Children Just Like You; There Once Was a World: A Nine Century Chronicle of the Shtetl of Eishyshok;* and *The Liberators: Eyewitness Accounts of the Liberation of Concentration Camps.*

Photo Credits

Series Design
Kim Sonsky

Layout
Laura Murawski